BOOK

OF

POEMS

II

by DeArrius D. Rhymes

TABLE OF CONTENTS

PRELUDE	Why I do What I do	3
CHAPTER I SPIRITUALLY	GOD IS	5
	OMG!	8
	Lord of ALL – Omi-	9
	Anesthesia	10
	Soul = Rhythm + Blues	11
	Afraid	12
	Resurrection Night	13
	Crucifying Him	15
	to Die is Gain	16
	and He Taketh Away	17
	A Fervent Prayer	18
	PRAISE HIM!!!	20
CHAPTER II MENTALLY	Dis•ease	22
	Optimism!	24
	In my head	25
	Who am I…	26
	Available	27
	It matters	28
	Jane, Mary	29
CHAPTER III PHYSICALLY	Hometown	31
	Bathsheba	32
	GTS	33
	Cadaver	34
	LH 122	35
	Divided	36
	Cutting Grass – MME	37

CHAPTER IV	Heartbroken	39
EMOTIONALLY	Let em go	41
	a Real, Good Man…	42
	Enough?	44
	Greener grass	45
	Cliché	46
	June Third Two Thousand Twenty-Four	48
CHAPTER V	ALL vanity	50
NATURALLY	No•thing	51
	No doubt	52
	Pain / Pleasure	53
	Good person	54
	Un[der]*appreciated.*	55
	unnaturaL	56
CHAPTER VI	The American Dream	58
ETHNICALLY	Read n Write	60
	Five hundred dollar bills	61
	color blindness	62
	Courtesy	63
	~~Nigger~~ Proud ~~Boys~~ Men	64
	4 Notes	65
CHAPTER VII	I AM!	67
PERSONALLY	Doctor Dee	68
	Surprise!!!	69
	April Second Two Thousand Twenty-Two	70
	King Dee	72
	Being Great: Climb On	73
	When the heart stops	74
POSTLUDE	Aftermath	75

PRELUDE

Why I do What I do

    I believe I have good things to say; words I believe are more than worthy of being shared with others in need of hearing them.

Whether it be to unbolt and open the hearts and minds of people or to simply encourage those who need encouragement, sharing my divulged gift of writing and the wisdom that I'm fortunate to have brings me great joy!

To that point, for those who have my first Book of Poems, thank you for your loving support; you're in for a treat! If you have not obtained a copy, I highly recommend that you do, as this piece intentionally complements it innumerably in style and nature.

    Ultimately, I do not write primarily for money, fame, or personal gain, but rather for the benefit of those who choose to read and hopefully be able to apply my words to particular situations in life.

    #ToGodBeTheGlory

CHAPTER I

SPIRITUALLY

GOD IS

GOOD is not just an adjective to positively describe our days here on Earth or the *better* things we experience in life. Good is how we feel when we deliberately take moments to not be negligent of God's daily blessings and appreciate them, even if our current personal circumstances are not aligned in our favor.

ALL the time we confuse God's goodness with the not-so-good things we are going through. We forget that God is All-powerful; that He sees all, knows all, and has already worked out all our future situations, even before allowing our mother to be formed in our grandmother's womb!

THE God that created the universe by word of mouth and saw that it was "Good" is the same God that lovingly and intentionally crafted us by hand in His own, perfect image! So, before doubting God's goodness, reminisce on His infinite record of awesome and majestic things He has performed since the beginning…

TIME is a creation of God and, furthermore, a matter of higher thinking. People use the phrase, "Since the beginning of time" without thinking twice about when its beginning really was. Before God put it in place, there was no such thing as time–something our human minds cannot begin to comprehend. Yet, God saw that it would be good to provide chronological structure.

AND to that point, it is interesting how we find ways to put a limit on the amount of time that God, the creator of it, has to invoke a drastic change in our lives. Do you not realize that God could stop time and start it back without us even knowing it happened? Can you fathom the fact that God never sleeps because He alone is above time itself? So, be patient and understand, in due time, He will allow good to occur in your favor.

ALL of us can recount a time in our lives when God was good, because He is good all the time! You see, God being good all the time is not dependent upon everything going right in your life. But behold, it means that no matter what He allows to happen in your life, He only means it for the greater good!

THE worst thing we can do is wallow in our sorrows... You were fired from a job that didn't appreciate you. You might be unemployed for months as a testament to your faith. Then right before your breaking point, God blesses you with the ultimate job that you enjoy; that pays you twice as much as you were once making. And after this experience, someone else is able to benefit from your testimony.

TIME allows us to benefit from the boundless grace and mercy of God that ultimately inclines us to yield ourselves to Him. For example, of course, God is good and praiseworthy when everything in life is going right; you are healthy, and doing well day by day. But, what about when the grandmother you love so dearly passes away or when you can't seem to pass the exam needed to get into the school or be hired for the job you desire? Is God not the same gracious and merciful One that allowed you time with grandma or to even have the opportunity to take the test or have the job interview? Is God not good anymore?

GOD IS, in fact, still good, and even then He is worthy to be praised! As a matter of fact, God allows you to stoop to your lowest point in order to cause a positive spiritual feedback reaction. Instead of letting what we are experiencing in the present realm of our life affect our spirit, we should say, "God, I believe but help thou mine unbelief," and start rejoicing and praising and thanking God in advance for what is about to transpire in our lives, in due time.

GOOD is loving God and our neighbors as Jesus commanded us, and doing our best to live right in every circumstance! When we are weak, good is turning back to God after losing your way; and then helping your loved-ones and enemies to do the same when you are strong! Good is trusting in the Lord who sent His only son, Jesus, to save us, so that we might be able to live with Him in eternal peace and heavenly luxury after having endured this journey!

OMG!

Oh my God, how Marvelous is Your name!
Mighty are Your works and wonders. You, my
God, are awesome, and Holy are Your ways.

Occasionally I often wonder, how do You do it all?
More than anything, what makes You do it all?
God help me to understand, even if only a portion!

Oftentimes You send storms and wars my way. And in the midst of them, it seems as if You just want to blow me away or wouldn't care if I died on the battlefield.
Make no mistake, I understand I have to go through trials and tribulations; I know that being saved doesn't make the journey easier. But, oh my
God, now I get it! The storms were sent to overthrow those against me, and in the process, help me to grow and strengthen my roots. And the war was allowed so I could see that I never have to fight a battle because I have You!

On the God I serve, I put it on everything I love… You, Jesus, and the Holy Spirit within me are all I truly need to conquer this life.
Most importantly, I realize developing a closer bond with You is the key to my sanity, peace, hope, joy, and success!
Grateful is an understatement and thankful is the the least I'll forever be for all the known and unknown You do on my behalf.

Lord of ALL – Omni-

I wonder who He is?
Who is He that does it ALL by
turning nothing into everything?

Some say an explosion with
unimaginable force created matter,
propelling it outward to make billions of galaxies.

I simply believe it was Him,
the eternal God of the universe and
ALL creation, that said, "Let there be light."

The Lord of ALL:
Mr. "I Am That I Am"; that's
who I've established Him to be!

Omnipotent:
With all power in Your hands, I don't have to worry about what
the future holds, since You hold me in the palm of Your hands.

Omnipresent:
Everywhere I go, I never worry about anything, especially
being encompassed by danger, because I know You are there.

Omniscient:
You know everything there is to know because You are the
orchestrator and Lord of ALL!

Anesthesia

Is it not amazing to you: God performing the first surgery?
Sleep Adam, rest well. Because once you wake up
Only I have foreseen the perfect gift that you'll have.
For out of the rib of man, the Lord chose to make woman.
Let's think about this for a moment. Without a doubt,
Unequivocally speaking, God is all we need! Yet, I
Recall Him directly saying, "It is not good for the man to be
Alone; I will make him a helper suitable for him."
Nonetheless, succeeding this prodigious event, there would
Eventually come the fall of mankind, as a result of free will.

Don't think for one second my God wasn't prepared or didn't
Already know what would take place out of disobedience! Yet,
Not even Satan's devices could counteract the stupendously
Tremendous plan the Father, Son, and Holy Spirit executed to
Repair what would've been eternal malignant hyperthermia;
Only God could save us from the eternal damnation ahead,
Like an incessant nightmare coupled with a bolus of ketamine!
Everything is okay now though because Lucificer lost! So
Now, we can sleep peacefully, knowing God has reserved
Each of us, who accepts Jesus, a postoperative bed in Heaven!

Soul = Rhythm + Blues

Lord, I tried it on my own.
But I see that *I'm going down*
when You ain't around!
And now, my whole world's upside!

I'm *Lost Without U*.
I can't help myself!
But how does it feel
to know that I love You, Jesus!

Lord, now that I'm saved, *teachme* how to love.
Show me the ways to surrender my heart. God, I'm so lost!
Teach me how to love; how I can get my Spirit involved.
Teach me how to love!

I realized *I don't wanna* be without You, be without You!
I don't wanna live without You, live without You;
I don't wanna go without You, go without You;
Lord, I don't wanna be alone–separated from You!

Afraid

God, I'm afraid, so afraid; I'm
afraid of becoming too close to You.
Because I can hear you so clearly, and,
in my humanity, I'm afraid I'll mess us up.

I'm afraid to read Your words because You
are the Word. And, if I understand it, then
I understand You. Then, if my ways don't
align with Yours, I'll have to make changes.

I'm afraid to remain consistent and be on fire
for You at all times; I'm afraid to always let my
Light shine! Because, when my fire goes out and
my light becomes dim, will I still be worth loving?

I realized, as a child, *in Spirit* and in truth, that I
undoubtedly want to come to Heaven with You.
But that was especially because, to tell You the truth,
I was more so afraid of going to Hell for eternity.

But behold… Now, God, I'm afraid, so afraid; I'm
scared of being without You! How could I live *in
Peace*? Who would guide me as You have? Who would I
become, considering the lengths I'd go in my humanity?

Verily, verily, I proclaim, now, I'm more afraid of not
being too close to you! I'm afraid of neither understanding
You, knowing Your ways, nor changing mines too! And, I'd
be petrified, more so, if I could not spend forever praising You!

Resurrection Night

Hallelujah, Selah,
The Savior *lives*!
Eternity is mines cause,
now, Hell and Death must yield!

Rejoice, rejoice, Amen!
All power is in His hands!
Behold His Glory tonight,
as Satan cries and replans!

I praised Him and shouted
this morning; I just couldn't help it!
Cause, when I think of Him walking
outta that tomb, my soul gets excited!

As a result, I have hope,
And I'm forever covered!
I can come to Him in all my times of
trouble, all because He conquered!

I mean, just imagine Jesus
grieving on his knees in Gethsemane;
Asking God, "Is this the only way?" Then
choosing to accept His fate, all for me!

He was spat on, made fun of, whipped until disfigured,
nailed, and still forgiving, even while hung!
Cause, He knew, lest I be left behind when the trumpet
sounds, I'd need Him when the time comes!

Hallelujah, Rejoice,
My Savior lives!
Eternity is mines, all because
He holds All Power and forgives!

April 9, 2023, 11 PM

Crucifying Him

You might not have beaten me,
      spat on me, mocked or made fun
            of me, or nailed me to that cross.

But, you crucify me every day when you don't choose me.

      Did you think when I asked my Father
            to "Forgive them for they know not what
                  they do" that you weren't included too?

to Die is Gain

Why am I here?
I mean I guess I have a purpose, but I could care less…
sometimes.

I agree that every day
is not supposed to be peaches and cream. But, does that mean
bad days have to be rotten peaches and spoiled cream?

Life can be very burdensome. And, no,
I'm not suicidal, but I mean, come on… If I have done all the
good I feel I was assigned to do, what is left for me here?

And I found the answer
to the question: nothing. There is nothing left
here for me, or at least nothing I think.

But behold, my Brother has a plan for me:
for, to live is Christ. So, with that in mind, I'll go to bed and
try to look forward to tomorrow. Lord, *I'm Available to You!*

And if I'm not here
in this weary land, on this side of eternity,
when I wake up, I won't be mad; for I have gained.

But if I'm still here,
I'll know that the purpose I have fulfilled is not enough. For I
must fulfill His full purpose for me; then He'll call me home.

and He Taketh Away

I'm showered in blessings.
I'm content in my lavishness.
I'm delighted to be shined on by the Son.

But, I know the day will come:
A day when I must give up my everything; a day
even before being lowered six feet below ground.

And on that day, what shall I say?
Shall I cry, stomp and pout in indignation?
Shall I sob until my anger goes away?

Or, will I be content in my forced haplessness?
Will I still praise and remember: the same One
that giveth hath the right to taketh away.

Moreover, when it's my season again,
I'll understand my duty.
As a result of suffering… I'll appreciate the phase.

> I'm showered in blessings; therefore, I bless others.
> I'm content in my lavishness, after giving abundantly.
> I'm delighted to be shined on by the Son and to be a light.

A Fervent Prayer

Father God, I come in the Name of Jesus, thanking You for today; thanking You for waking me up this morning, for keeping me up to this present moment, and for all that You're going to do today–even if it is Your will that my time on this Earth must end before this day is over!

Lord, I pray that You go before me today and clear my path! Wrap me in your loving arms of protection; nonetheless, should I endure tragedy today, I pray that You keep me through it! And last but not least, I pray that You have a great day today as well!

Master, I ask that You please forgive me for my sins of omission and commission, whether done in word, thought, or deed – spiritually, mentally, physically, emotionally, or in any other way form of fashion! Forgive your people for their sins, and even forgive those who don't know you in the pardon of their sins, for they know not what they do!

Jehovah, I ask You to please bless the things I do today; so much so that the people I interact with and the things I associate myself with produce quality products of gold, only if it glorifies You; that my spiritual tree might yield delicious fruit pleasing in Your site!

Most High, I pray for my present and future family and friends, and even more importantly, I pray for my enemies, known and unknown; that you bless them all willfully and abundantly in Jesus's Name!

Sweet Savior, I thank you for sending your Son, Jesus, to die on the cross for my sins! If I had ten thousand tongues I couldn't thank You enough for the multitudinous, incalculable debt You paid when You saved me by the Blood of my big Brother, Jesus.

Awesome is Your Name; with a heart parallel to that of David, I declare that You are worthy to be praised! Wonderful are Your works; Holy are Your words; Matchless is Your sufficient grace and mercy and the peace you give us! This prayer, I humbly submit to You, in the Name of Jesus, Amen!

PRAISE HIM!!!

Praise Him,
praise Him, praise Him!!!

Praise Him,

PrAiSe Him, pRaIsE Him!!!

Praise Him, Praise Him, Praise Him!!!

PRAISE Him, PRAISE Him,

PRAISE HIM!!!

In Every Aspect And in Total Reverence, HE MUST BE PRAISED!!!

Chapter II

Mentally

Dis•ease

Every disease begins in your mind,
especially for victims of negative thinking
who perpetually fight from behind.

Many will quit fighting before even fighting the
fight, and even, more give up trying before trying to
try. "You'll always fail!" is a lie; yet, you'll always
fail if you never try!

For, a disease can cause you dis-ease because you're
worried about your fate. Then your dis-ease fuels
your disease when you believe you've fallen from
grace and mercy.

Your mind plays a huge role in it all – I can't say it
enough! Your mind plays a huge role in it all, until
you say that's enough!

Positive thinking is a daily practice; a good day and
a bad day are basically the same. For, you
conquered yesterday's trails. The only difference is
today's issues are bringing you pain.

The key is to have faith in the best that's yet to come
because today's faith yields tomorrow's blessings
after the race has been run.

Whether it is a thing or a person, whether it be
cancer or depression, understand life's journey is

never-ending, so you'll always be dis-eased in some fashion. However, don't amplify the lesson. Just remember there's a blessing. Release your worries, and your disease will lose its suppression.

These rhymes may seem sweet and nice to read, but they'll mean anything if you don't take heed to get up off the ground and stand on your feet. I believe you can win, and I want to see you make it; your test will soon become your testimony!

Optimism!

Be positive; please, be positive! Thinking positively is not merely a mindset but rather a way of living.

Think happy thoughts; please, think happy thoughts! True happiness is a stem of internal joy; "Don't we all want that?"

Be content in bad situations; please, be content in bad situations! Just because life is not going the way you intend, does not mean it is not panning out for your good and in your favor.

Be cheerful; please, be cheerful! You never know who may be watching you and who depends on you to brighten their day.

Let go of negativity; please, let go of negativity! If being negative takes you anywhere, it will only be backwards.

So, be positive; please, be positive! Trade out your pessimism for optimism, and I promise you "Life will never be bad."

In my head

Up here, in this dome of mine,
I can say anything I want, and I
don't have to give an account for it...
At least not to you!

Oh, lemme be the first to tell ya,
"Up here, ain't no limits!" And uhh,
sorry in advance, even though you can't
hear what's going on up here.

I mean, I can really show out, up here.
I can always make things clear!
Man watchu say? If you don't gectho...
I mean, really set the record straight.

Up here, I can tell ole girl exactly how I feel,
then, I can send to the lips what I want to reveal,
after filtering everything else that wasn't
designed for the atmosphere to witness.

In my head, I can control the narrative!
I can make it all dull or infinitely creative.
Because, up here, my truth lies,
and it's up to *us* to set it free.

Who am I...

... to judge you
For what you've been
through, when I, too,
Have my own issues?

... to not forgive you,
For the wrong you've done,
as if I've done no wrong
And am the perfect one?

... to not show everybody love,
Regardless of how I'm treated,
whether I'm having an awesome day
Or one when I'm defeated?

Who would I be...

Available

What's the point in me telling you how I actually feel?

I mean I'm not afraid to share my feelings, but it's almost pointless if you're not going to comfort me or have even the slightest response with a milligram of sincere meaning.

So, nahh. I'd rather just keep it all in.

I can pray it out, or talk to someone who does care
or, more desirably, will have something to say back.

And no need for jealousy.

I'm not looking for someone to give me a specific response;
I'm not asking for something you're not capable of giving.
I'm simply in need of what your negligence is allowing.

It matters

Sometimes a pen doesn't matter
    until you need to write something.

Sometimes a pencil doesn't matter
    until you need to be able to erase something.

Sometimes one's life does not matter
    until it's gone.
    But why wait till then?

Sometimes food won't matter
    until you've been without it.

Sometimes a grade won't matter
    until it's an F.

Sometimes resources will not matter
    until they're gone.
    But why get to that point?

In order for something to truly matter,
    must we eventually go without from time
    to time, even if we already know from previous
    experiences what it's like to go without, in general?

Jane, Mary

Haha… wait, why am I laughing?
Was that even funny?
Chill out man; you trippin'!
Pass.

Stomach growls … that's tough.
I'm hungry with something to eat.
Crazy way to starve.
Pass.

This ain't even me… literally.
Who is you and who are mes¿
I need some water, please.
Pass.

Cough, cough … that's wild.
All this oxygen around, and I can't breathe .
Where's air when you need it?
Pass.

I'm… done with this mess.
After this I am.
Haha, for real.
I'm good.

Chapter III

Physically

Hometown

Though I may be gone,
You will always be my home.
For you taught me many
Lessons to use along the way.

    So many lessons, I can't keep track.
    So many friends who turned their backs.
    And even then I came back, especially
    (Only) for the loyal ones who awaited me.

I left to come back, yet I didn't come
Back to stay. For, I've acquired some
New qualities that have habituated
Me to a newly discovered, fine taste.

    So, although this is my forever-home,
    This is not where I will forever-belong.
    I've gone off for the better, I returned
    For the better, and I'll leave for better.

Humbly, I'm not "too good" for this place,
but I'm worth more in another space.
Can't you see, I'm about to elevate my
Game to bring us both to greater heights.

    So, don't trip over the choices I make;
    Don't gossip about the roads I'll take.
    Respectfully, be fair to me as a proud
    Native of this town, the town I call home.

October 2021

Bathsheba

My, my, my! Somebody, please,
join me in adoring
this fine beauty that would adorn me!

I mean, look at her headlights;
look at her rear end.
I can only imagine how smoothly she rides.

And when the roads get rough,
I bet she'd hold me down
no matter how hard I push or the miles I put on her.

Oh, how fresh and how sweet
she must be on the inside.
How warm and cozy I'd be in the winter time.

She must feel my eyes on her,
that gorgeous frame.
A masterpiece; if painted, only once, never to be again.

I can't do it anymore; I must have her!
Whatever the price, I'll pay!
If nothing else is for sure, she's coming with me today!

#SHEBADD

GTS

What you doing?
Where you at?
What you about to do?
Oh, okay.

Well, I was thinking…
Yeah, I know…
I don't care though…
Ok, I understand.

Well, just let me know,
if something changes.
I'm just sitting here,
bored in my loneliness.

Well, it's fine then…
Honestly, it's all good…
It's really not worth it…
To sleep I go.

Cadaver

Here you go; use me! I'm here to help you,
don't you see?

I know it's hard to connect right now,
but, soon, as you get to know me,
we'll make memories you'll never forget!

6 feet below ground? Nahh, why do that
when I can rest above ground.

Just submerge me instead; I'm a fan of
this formaldehyde stuff. It keeps me looking
just as good as I hope to by this point.

Do what you have to, I understand.
I'd rather trust you with me to prepare you
when one's life is in your hands.

Learn all that you can, and don't take any
of it for granted.

By the way, you owe me for this; you have to prove
me right to those who doubted my brave decision.

My autonomy is beyond your delicate care;
show the world that, even now, I can still
teach tangible lessons and give to others
in a way that extends the time beyond
that which I was granted.

LH 122

    I love it here!
        I hate it here!
    I can't wait to be there!
        When will I ever leave?

        I feel dumb here.
        I continuously fail here.
    I'm smarter than I was!
    I'm succeeding day by day!

    I'm on the right track!
        I wanna turn back…
        There's no light in sight.
    Can't give up now!

        No windows, like a jail.
    Assembled with panoramic detail;
    A beautiful, resourceful place!
        Surrounded, yet isolated.

        Set the negatives aside…
    You worked to be here, and
    you were also chosen to be here!
    You belong here!

Divided

Half of me wants to hear what you're saying,
but the other half doesn't care at all.

"Can I have your undivided attention?"
Of course! You have about 10 to 20 seconds.

I'm here, but my countenance should let you know
that I unintentionally left nearly an hour ago.

Why do we expect to "come together"
when everything has been separated.

Lucifer deceived and took a third of the angels from Heaven!
And you expect this earthly congregation to be fully united?

If one has a stroke, doesn't only half of the face droop or
become numb or one side of the body's muscles weaken?

Not to say division is the final result; of course, it's not.
But on that same token, some division is necessary.

To either have night all day or day all night would derange us;
or having to turn on all the stove eyes to boil a pot of noodles.

"I could be around *you* all day!" *Are you sure about that?*
Half of me loves that, but sometimes I've gotta get away.

Cutting Grass – MME

As an African American male, I am very fortunate to have a great father who is actively present in my life, and having the opportunity to cut lawns with him has edified my life in ways unimaginable.

Over the years, the hard work and labor that comes with cutting grass has become second nature. In the midst of rain, early mornings, the noonday's blazing sun, and whatever the day yields, the job must be completed. I have learned to be more long-suffering, versatile, and dedicated to the task in ideal and non-ideal environments and circumstances.

Beyond the physical aspect, I also love being able to channel my inner thoughts and spirit. This experience caused me to gain a distinct appreciation for nature in a unique fashion while allowing me to participate in maintaining the health of the earth. Moreover, I believe turning properties from a mess to a masterpiece symbolizes "restoration." For me, it is synonymous with the work of physicians, who aid in the healing and restoring of health in patients; there is instant gratification, like administering anesthesia.

Additionally, cutting lawns has been a financial help as well. It has given me the money to not only have for myself but to also use for wholesome endeavors. Some of it I use to fund the scholarships I award at Hazlehurst High School, and it was the primary source that granted me the ability to publish my first "Book of Poems."

AMCAS, 1 of 3 MMEs

Chapter IV

Emotionally

Heartbroken

I know a person who unintentionally broke someone's heart as a result of previously being heartbroken themselves. It's a cycle, don't you see!

I know that guard you have up is a shield you once carried by your side and never thought of, until your atria and ventricles were punctured. Now, you've put a price on your unconditional love, that was once free.

Let's deal with this pain, reverse the cycle, and change the game because I'm sick and tired of being stuck and uninspired. Sick and tired indeed.

First, take a breath and admit to yourself you're not who you used to be. You used to have colorful autumn leaves that never fell, but then you became like all the other evergreens.

You're rightfully afraid to show what you truly believe; real love is real, and you know it! They played with your feelings; now you're playing with your feelings and scared of being happy.

Love is peace, not confusion; so, don't confuse them. Why accept being mistreated, betrayed, and abused when you can sail out of the Sea of Perplexity?

The reason is that you see another person in the cycle, damaged like you, with equal potential. However, it's important that you know, you can't deliver someone who doesn't want to *be*.

So, this is what you do: take care of you, and don't give up by trying again. And when the going gets tough, don't fall to the ground shattered in tears; instead, get on your knees.

Ask the Creator of strength for the ability to love again, for He knows the struggle! And if you don't have the strength to ask for it, simply sigh, "Father, help me please…"

Things are going to come together in your favor if you trust the process. Every storm passes in due time, and if you can just hang on, you'll repair your broken heart and conquer this cycle – I guarantee!

Let em go

I know it's hard
to let em go!
But the sooner you do it,
The sooner you'll know…

You're worth more
than you're settling for.
But you'll never realize that,
until you walk out the door.

Whether it's that man or woman,
even a parent, or your best friend,
losing hair and sleep over whomever
will not be worth it in the end.

Be fair to yourself;
why not be happy?

a Real, Good Man…

"Happy wife, happy life,"
but what about the Man?
    For everything he sacrifices,
    should his happiness be bland?
        I'm not talking about just anyone,
        but a Real, Good Man…
            After everything he sacrifices,
            why must his happiness be bland?

While you sleep peacefully,
he's making sure you're safe.
    And if anything pops off,
    he's running to save the day.
        I'm not talking about just anyone,
        but a Real, Good Man…
            Because if anything pops off,
            he's already got a plan.

When the tab is too high to pay,
yet, and still, he pays it with ease.
    Not because he had it to spend,
    but merely to keep you pleased.
        I'm not talking about just anyone,
        but a Real, Good Man…
            Because he doesn't have it, but
            what matters is that you can.

So, what about his joy and peace?
Will you be that for him?
    Can you vow to make his day easier?
    Is he deserving or just "another one of them?"
        I'm not talking about just anyone,
        but a Real, Good Man…
            Will you vow to make his life easier
            because he is your Real, Good Man?

Enough?

Is enough ever enough?
I mean really: will enough, finally, ever, really be enough?

Like when I go above and beyond…
Is it that you want more, or is what I'm doing just not enough?

Imagine expressing your appreciation and admiration for
someone with infinite "I love you"s and back-breaking actions
to prove, solidify, and reassure your feelings…
Now imagine being asked, "Is your love for me really true?"

Huh?
Shaking my head; What… Do… You… Mean!?

What more can be done, to please you!?
Is there an actual answer, or is doing or being enough
just my never-ending, hallucinated fantasy?

Greener grass

Is it worth it?
Probably so…

But, it'll only be worth it
until you're back
where you are now.

So, is it worth it?
Yeah, probably so…

But, always remember,
the grass you have was
once *your* greener grass!

The other grass may
definitely be greener!

But, all grass can be
green, and all grass
has times when it's not.

Cliché

I love you… "I love you."
Oh no, I said it!
What was I thinking?
How could I be so reckless!?

"Oh, really?" she asks.
"Oh yes, I mean it!"
Shaking my head!
I hope I don't regret it.

You shouldn't have said it.
You know what they say.
I asked, "Do you love me?"
She hesitates…

It was too early, way too early!
What an idiot!
She smirks and says,
"I was afraid you'd never ask."

My heart is pounding!
What does that mean?
Does she–
"I love you too!"

Whew, I knew it, I knew it!
Forget what they say.
"I nearly began to believe
that saying it was cliché."

With passion she states,
**"It's never cliché,
as long as you mean it!"**
Wow… that's interesting.
"I never *thought* of it that way."

"Well, I love you, and I mean it;
and I'll say it every day!"
She blushes; I kiss her.
Our love is not cliché!

June Third Two Thousand Twenty-Four

I wasn't sure where life would take us... My hopes and desires were merely to take every next step we made together.

At the beginning, I really thought you would be different; I honestly thought we could make it! I wanted to be the man of your dreams and write a story so seemingly unreal that we would have to testify about its nonfiction nature.

Behold, after a few trips around the sun, I can honorably say the hopes, desires, and thoughts were real! It's amazing how, when real love felt so unachievable and out of reach, God aligned our paths in His own perfect way.

Have I been perfect? No, and as sure as we continue to live and grow together, we will have our days. And although I may not be perfect, I thank you for "making me complete" by being my other half. *I Believe in You and Me.*

Inspired by my **Love for Her**
Est. June 3, 2021

Chapter V

Naturally

ALL vanity

The houses, the cars,
the clothes, and shoes…

The money, the drinks,
the drugs, and sex…

The lavish vacations, the five-star dining,
the parties, and careers we pursue…

                                     … it's ALL vanity.

No•thing

There is nothing, literally no-thing, you can do to ultimately please a person.

    You can travel the world to the most romantic place on earth with the one you love, and wine and dine the entire time to cement the most unforgettable moments in his or her heart.
    Then a single sentence can change the entire atmosphere and uproot all the genuine work you did for that person.

You can do everything asked of you to perfection; but how long does perfection last?

    Try cleaning every square foot of the house from the floor to the ceiling, and washing dishes, and folding clothes, and taking out the trash, and whatever else is needed.
    Then what happens to your credit when a spec of dirt is found by someone; the same someone who happened to be wearing shoes?

Understand nothing lasts forever, and no-thing can be done to change that!

    A beautiful couple of 50 years; the husband dies and the wife cries because she knows there's no-thing anyone can do to fill the void.
    If the husband could've, he would've stayed, but there's nothing he could've done to make that change!

    Sometimes the answer is not simply nothing, but it is unfortunately no-thing…

No doubt

      Can one be narcissistic and humble – not simultaneously, but in general?

      Can one be loyal and faithful for 40 years, and not lose the trust of his or her partner after cheating the next day?

      Can I have 364 great days, yet be merely remembered for the one or two bad ones?

      Can one be innocent in copious ways, guilty in a couple, and then be persecuted forever simply for the two?

      Should someone, with no jurisdiction, judge somebody; does a Judge have the right to over-judge a person?

For if it be winter, and the grass be not green,
is it still not grass?

And if the water be not clear, or blue,
are its base components not still the same?

And if the firmament be filled with raining clouds throughout the day, is the un not still brightly shining somewhere above?

Pain / Pleasure

Temporary pain is better than temporary pleasure.
Yet, if you had to choose between the two,
Which would you desire?

Yeah, so don't fault me if I don't choose pain!
And don't call me crazy if I don't choose pleasure!

Is it not better to suffer in the present for future gain?
Then, in the future, only your past shall be the pain.

Don't eat it, don't beat it, don't treat it.
You don't need (to do) it!

Yeah, it's hard to wait, and pleasure's hard to hate!
But won't you feel pain at some point anyway?

No, that doesn't mean choose him or choose them *over* you.
But the pain, actually, is choosing yourself…

Pain or pleasure, which one will it be?
Denying you is always free.

Good person

Naturally, you'd imagine being a good person
gets you further in life.

I was taught that being trustworthy, loyal, helpful, friendly,
courteous, kind, obedient, cheerful, thrifty, brave, clean, and
reverent can get you anywhere in life.

And while all of that is fine and fantastic, without hard work,
being good will only get you so far!

Great people lose jobs, get shot, become homeless, have
declining health, grieve over past family and friends….
and even go to Hell – if their soul is lost.

So, how good of a person will you be, in efforts to live the best
life while living and the best life after death; is that possible?

Un[der]*appreciated.*

Thank you so much for
Everything you have done,
All that you're doing, and the
Things you will continue to do!!!

appreciated.

finally, it's about time…
thanks, I guess.

unnaturaL

Growth is natural…

But, sometimes, in order to grow,
    you must defy that which is normal,
comfortable, and expected of you.

    Remember, your
peculiarities set you
    apart from the rest.

So, when there's
    no other way to be different,
        .tnereffid eb ot yaw wen a revocsid

Chapter VI

Ethnically

The American Dream

Last night I had a dream, a lengthy nightmare I'd never
wish for anyone to have. In my dream:
> I was having a blast with my family and friends. Suddenly, one
> by one, we were kidnapped by pale-looking people.
> I was locked away on a huge something that was floating in the
> water; and after forever, I was finally taken off.
> But, I wasn't at home anymore, and for some reason, I had
> chains on my wrists and ankles.

I awoke out of my sleep. All was well, so I laid back down
and continued to dream:
> I was in a field picking white stuff out of some plants amongst
> hundreds of others like me. I stopped because
> I was tired and about to pass out, which led to me being
> wrapped across my back with something that brought me to
> my knees.

Sweating, I arose up again! But all was well, so I went
back to sleep. The dream continued, but it was better:
> I was able to walk around freely with no issues, and I received
> pay for the work I did throughout the day. Everything
> seemed normal.
> I went to buy food from some place called "GROCERIES FOR
> WHITES ONLY" on my way home from work. Upon entering,
> the people inside gave me a peculiar look and started calling
> me words I didn't understand, "Mother– " something and
> a word that rhymes with bigger.

The next thing I knew, I was out cold; and I woke up high off
the ground, fighting to breathe, and surrounded by a crowd of
people cheering, who looked similar to the
ones in the marketplace.

Gasping for air, I woke up immediately! I looked out the
window, and it was still dark. I tried to stay up out of fear
of another dream, yet, exhausted, I couldn't help it.
Asleep I fell:
    Somehow, someway, I ended up at a shindig with smoke in the
air. Everywhere I went people were nice, even *those* from my
previous dreams.
    I was offered a cup of something, and thirstily, I drank it. My
chest got hot and the room started to spin. Next thing I knew
there were back-to-back "booms" and "bangs" and everyone
scattered. Stumbling over my feet and others, I managed to get
out of the building.
    As I hobbled out, I was blinded by bright lights, and instantly,
my body was redirected to the ground by what felt like
constant fire slicing through my body. As things began to fade
out, all I could hear was, "Put your hands–."

I jumped out of my bed, and got on my knees! I prayed,
and I prayed more for relief! Thank God it was only a
dream. Safe and sound was I as the break of dawn began
to creep through the window.
    I walked outside to get some cool, fresh air from the sweet
breeze of the Atlantic sea. Then, as I gazed over the beautiful
West African beach, in the distance, I noticed something huge
in the distance, floating in the water – coming, almost,
I think, directly towards me…

Read n Write

I'd love'ta learn
how'ta read n write
if' Ah could…

But Ah'jus can't;
I can showl speak that good
Massa-talk tho.

B'sides
Ah'heard issa'gainst
tha law anyways…

Or a'least
Massa don't wan'it
happenin'.

Five hundred dollar bills

Five hundred dollars is a pretty sweet lil penny if you're broke. Count it out a one-dollar bill at a time, and it'll take you a precious amount of time.

Compare pennies to days, months to dimes, and years to dollars; five hundred years is a pretty sweet lil penny.

Fourscore and seven years of grueling work accounts for three or four generations. So, I wonder how many generations four hundred sweet, lil ole years of slavery accounted for?

So tell me... was reconstruction supposed to heal slavery? Or maybe a good ole five hundred dollars worth of land; "surely that holds infinite value in today's time!"

Then Mister Crow and Mister Sam found a way to make it happen; mass incarceration equals modern day slavery and taxes rob those who slave to make ends meet.

You read this, and don't agree? Oh, well let's see...
The poor pay taxes that build penitentiaries, which house free laborers who are being punished for their wrong acts. African Americans are not the only ones enslaved, yet the ratios by percentages are disproportionate.

color blindness

Only in America can we be integrated yet segregated... but not wholly admit that we're still divided; then embrace the truth to do something about it. Sitting in the same class, being served at the same restaurant, enjoying life at the same party: gathered together, yet still managing to group up and live separately.

Really the burden falls on us all, regardless of the race or background. However, the Civil Rights movement was not only as successful as it was merely because of the many great Negros that led it, but also because of the good Whites who chose to embrace truth by finally standing up for what's morally right!

Getting a Bachelor of Science in Chemistry and Master of Science in Biomedical Sciences and completing my first year towards obtaining a Doctor of Medicine degree from the University of Mississippi has shown me a lot. Ole Miss became New Miss when it was subsequently desegregated in 1962 by veteran James H Meredith via the overriding order of President JFK...

Ever since, folks of all races, other than those originally granted the privilege, have been able to benefit from receiving knowledge from the Gatekeeper of it. Yet, no minorities, besides same-race victims, have genuinely shown Mr. Meredith appreciation for the privileged opportunity to receive a White-only education.

Not going to lie... it's really sad: the outcome of most situations in America! Even after prolonged progress, many people who could be the further change are color-blinded by black-and-white depictions that portray history as inconsistent with our present circumstances.

Courtesy

A cough and a sneeze,
"Sir, we're gonna have to ask you to leave!"
What did I do wrong?
Am I not human?

    Surely I am! All humans sneeze, right?
    Right. Now, let's transition…

A burger and a drink,
"Don't you know to go to the back, Boy? Think!"
What did I do wrong?
I thought I was a human.

    I know I'm human because I look like you!
    Let's take it a step further…

A book and a teacher,
"Come to this school, and you'll be under a bleacher!"
Education is a common courtesy.
Are we both not humans?

~~Nigger~~ Proud ~~Boys~~ Men

"Look, Ma! Look!
I finally got it!"

That's alright there, Baby! You deserve it n more!

"You ain't lyin'! But this ain't it!
I think imma go back, and get another one!"

We believe in you, Baby! Jus pray n never give up!

"How could I give up, after all y'all don did?
If it wasn't for God n all y'all did back in da day,
I couldn't have made it this far!"

Boy, what you mean "all y'all did?" You worked for this!

"Yeah, I did work hard for it, fasho.
But Ma, if it wasn't for y'all's sacrifice I–"

**Hey, hey, hey... You... earned... this!
And don't ever let nobody tell you nothin' different!
God did it, you earned it, n we's be proud of you, son!**

"Yes ma'am, I got you. Well, this degree is
for everybody, especially you n Pop!"

4 Notes

Congratulations on being accepted into the best medical school in the nation! Here, at the University of Mississippi Medical Center, we are a family, and we're looking forward to welcoming you into our School of Medicine family!

In addition to being excited, you should be very proud of yourself for this major accomplishment and milestone met!

I hope you're relaxing and enjoying life because the journey of a lifetime begins in August!

Chapter VII

Honestly

I AM!

Determined, distinguished and destined for greatness! I AM
An astounding achiever with many awesome qualities! I AM
Motivated to press forward, no matter the circumstance! I AM
Never dismayed, even though my naysayers want to see me fall!

Remarkable, respectable, resilient, and rich in spirit! I AM
Impeccable, incredible, insightful and very intelligent! I AM
Grateful for my life, all the good and bad, and I love me! I AM
Hardworking and headstrong; I am hopeful for my future! I AM
Talented and triumphant; a living testimony, uniquely created…

I AM!

Doctor Dee

Anything worth having aint easy.
Anything worth having is worth having though, right?

Blood, sweat, and tears…
All of them were shed at some point along the way!

What would you give to be the best–
Better than they've witnessed, than anyone might admit?

Imposter syndrome…
The result of extensive humility.

Pride is not what I'm full of;
It is what I have in my God who got me here.

What a joyous journey and time to be merry!
For my goals are favored, in that my steps have truly been
ordered down the path of ultimate academic Achievement!

And just as life vaporizes,
so shall the time between now and the day I am, hopefully,
afforded the grand honor of inducing my first patient.

Surprise!!!

"Huh!? What!?
OMGGG!!!
Thank y'all sooo
Very muchhh!!!"

Naw, for real, for real tho…
My support system…
Is Truly Amazing…
Like FRFR!!!

From Sammy, Vicki, and Samantha,
To *Her*, DuQuan, and honorary siblings,
To family, and close friends like Ahri and Fin.
Y'all are the ones; you all are
The people who motivate Dee!

    And, more properly speaking…
Because I understand who orders my steps,
I can truly be appreciative of everything
He's done to position me where *I AM!*

    So, in the future, I will be so much more thankful for the me that God has allowed me to become and who *I AM* through those who have invested in me via various aspects!
    Thank you beyond measure!!!

                                      #Berry's Seafood, 7/8/23

April Second Two Thousand Twenty-Two

"Achievement In Every Field of Human Endeavor,"
    Oh, what a phrase!
    Near and dear to the heart of many –
    some even praise!
Count it all joy because, trust and
    believe, spaces are few!
    For *every* road is long, rough, and rugged –
    even the road you think is smooth!

Help us, dear God, who judge what others do!
    For I'm nothing more than a
    son of You, a son of my father,
    a son of education, and a son of Diggs.

I realize, it ain't about what you think, but rather
    about what you make outta what
    you don't know. But, I also realize
    that many fear the unknown...

Every time one achieves, trust and
    believe, others will thwart!
    But, no worries, no worries, no worries at all.
    Just let them wait and wait forever on the fall.

Very proudly, I speak and say what I say…
> but, pride can get you killed on the battlefield.
> Nonetheless, I shall die someday; and, if it's over
> what I believe, I'll boldly enunciate what's true!

Everybody will have something to say anyway.
> So, hey, why not be who you were truly created
> to be. His assignment is the only one that matters
> anyway – I'm sure the Ten would say the same.

Many greats call, but few are chosen. The result
> of that… "Yo baby, yo baby, yo," sometimes
> becomes "Woah baby, oh baby, no!"

Even though there are many critiques,
> I truly thank the Man above for the journey,
> thus far, and for my unconquerable soul.

Nupe this, Nupe that; Kappa this, Kappa that.
> Kappa, Nupe; Nupe, Kappa…
> In Phi Nu Pi we all *should* stand.

The wise are few in number, no matter the group;
> it's a sad truth. Ultimately, as J H Meredith
> would declare, "Ain't no fool like an old fool."

UnKonKer4ble Paragon
#φνπ #B.A.N.S.'98
JA (MS), SPR '22

King Dee

When I look in the mirror, I see royalty.
I see a king with much in store.

> You may not see it, but that's okay.
> Someday, you will see a king!

> Listen, if the King of all Kings made me in
> His likeness, does that not make me a king-like?

Christ made me a joint heir to the kingdom, and
the Living Word says a crown is laid up for me.

> If you're looking for a royal court and a palace
> down here, your perception of royalty is flogged.

> High standards and serving all others, even if
> nothing else is accounted for, makes me a king.

Don't embellish my crown because
you can't see – or don't have – yours.

Being Great: Climb On

"Everybody says, 'I want to be great one day...'

"Well, first you have to decide what great is and then be that!

"All the people talk about is quitting; so much that they never get anything done!"

> I agree! Every human aspires to be great until they're met with the challenges designed to make them great.
>
> Remember, it's, especially, when you're just steps away from the peak of your Mount Everest that God's tests and Lucifer's slithery temptations may seem the toughest.
>
> At that point, you can likely expect greatness to be right around the corner… if you don't quit.
>
> So whatever you do…
> Keep climbing, no matter what, and never look back!
>
> *Inspired by* ***James H Meredith***

When the heart stops

When it's all over,
When it's all said and done,
What will be the result?

When your mental state comes to a halt,
And your emotions can no longer be felt by default…

When, physically, you're cold because
The final natural act has been performed…

When, ethnically, your status no longer matters
And who you honestly were will come into fruition…

When the only thing that matters is your spiritual being,
And the soul is either eternally blessed or damned…

When the heart stops,
And the end has come,
What will be your result?

POSTLUDE

Aftermath

        Where
      there's a
    one and two,
     shall there
      not then
       arise a
       three?

Made in the USA
Columbia, SC
02 September 2024